THE GROUP OF SEVEN
AND TOM THOMSON

Canada's most famous band of artists, their lives and times are presented with clarity and brevity in this small volume. The reader will enjoy a visual treasury of their work and gain an understanding of the historic and artistic development of these legendary figures.

THE McMICHAEL CANADIAN COLLECTION • KLEINBURG • ONTARIO

THE McMICHAEL CANADIAN COLLECTION

The McMichael Canadian Collection had a very personal beginning in the country home of Robert and Signe McMichael. After two decades it comprises Canada's largest public display of the art of Tom Thomson and the Group of Seven together with outstanding works of their contemporaries Emily Carr, Clarence Gagnon, David Milne and J. W. Morrice. Art of the Inuit, North-west Coast and Woodland Indian people is displayed in dramatic settings appropriate to their honoured place in Canadian artistic expression. Despite phenomenal growth, the Collection retains the very special quality achieved only by those who cherish the possessions in their care.

The two young Canadians built their country home near the delightful village of Kleinburg close to Metropolitan Toronto in 1954. They discovered a heavily wooded acreage and nestled their home on a crest overlooking a broad river valley. The unusual residence was built of old hand-hewn timbers with fireplaces of natural stone and enormous windows providing panoramas of the changing seasons. The McMichaels named their home "Tapawingo," an Indian word meaning "Place of Joy". This it has become to thousands of visitors to the gallery which is open every afternoon except Monday throughout the year.

In their early collecting years, the couple purchased their first two paintings, *Montreal River* by Lawren Harris and *Pine Island* by Tom Thomson. Their deep affection for distinctively Canadian art forms became an obsession and led them in pursuit of additional works. By 1964 their home had become a veritable Canadian treasure house and they believed that it should be available to all.

In 1965, the McMichaels gave their works of art, buildings, furnishings and land to the people of Canada in Right of the Province of Ontario. Since then they have, in partnership with the Ontario Government, continued to oversee the growing collection and its home. Now a thirty-two room structure faithfully following the founders' vision, the gallery houses a unique distillation of our nation's culture.

The Collection and surroundings reflect the McMichaels' intimate perception of the land they love. Theirs has always been an emotional dedication to Canada and an inspired confidence in the appreciation by her people of the heritage of the nation. Their dream has become a reality shared by Canadians of all ages and visitors from countries around the world.

From its beginnings as a small private effort, the Kleinburg Collection has grown to become an eloquent symbol of nationhood.

THE
GROUP OF SEVEN
AND
TOM THOMSON

TOM THOMSON
Woodland Waterfall   1916
123.0 x 132.5

Over fifty years ago, seven pioneering artists banded together in Toronto determined to change the course of Canadian art. MacDonald, Harris, Jackson, Lismer, Carmichael, Varley and Johnston called themselves the Group of Seven. The story of these artists together with their friend Tom Thomson, is one of men with the vision and strong desire to penetrate to the essence of the Canadian spirit. They provided a bold visual statement of this country while transcending the colonialism prevalent in her art circles. Theirs was a devotion to the ideal of an art rooted in nationalism.

In 1920, it was difficult to be a young Canadian artist unless one subscribed to the precepts of painting in the tradition favoured by the public and the Royal Canadian Academy. It was a romantic perception lacking the reality of the rough topography, the often hostile climate and dramatic change of season.

Harris, Jackson, Lismer, Varley and Carmichael studied in Europe and were familiar with the great heritage of historical and modern art. But they were determined to express something uniquely Canadian, and they searched for new forms and inspiration derived from the wilderness. Group of Seven painting was the product of a young nation where a minority of people were searching for their national identity. The Group artists found their solution through their own creativity based on the vast Canadian landscape.

At the same time as the men later to form the Group were gathering in Toronto, artists struggled with similar problems in Quebec and British Columbia. Emily Carr defied popular acceptance with her paintings of West-coast Indian villages and totems. Maurice Cullen and A. Y. Jackson successfully pioneered new techniques for painting the crisp atmosphere of Quebec winter days with the colours of shadow reflecting on the snow.

In January 1913, Lawren Harris and J. E. H. MacDonald travelled to Buffalo, New York to study an exhibition of contemporary Scandinavian art. The two artists felt an immediate affinity with these northern painters, and they returned to Toronto reaffirmed in their determination to break with the conventional traditions existing in Canadian art.

Five months later, Alexander Young Jackson arrived in Toronto. A gregarious, frankly outspoken person who regaled his companions with stories embellished with his lively sense of humour, he was equally at home with prospectors or statesmen.

Born in Montreal in 1882, family circumstances forced the young lad to leave school at twelve to work with a lithographing company. Jackson studied art in Paris at the Académie Julian from 1907 to 1909 and seemed more impressed with his associates than with the instruction. He travelled widely absorbing the European art scene.

Shortly after his return to Canada, Jackson exhibited what was to become a landmark canvas, *Edge of the Maple Wood* painted in 1910. MacDonald wrote to the artist in Emileville, Quebec, concerning the painting and significantly Jackson observed,

> *I began my association with the artists responsible for changing the course of Canadian art for many years to come.*

Jackson travelled to Berlin, Ontario, later named Kitchener, to visit relatives and during a stopover in Toronto, he met MacDonald, Arthur Lismer and Fred Varley at the Arts and Letters Club beginning long friendships. Lawren Harris was anxious to meet Jackson, and he journeyed to Berlin to discuss burgeoning ideas for the future.

A. Y. JACKSON
First Snow Algoma   1920
107.4 x 127.7

In January 1914, Jackson and Tom Thomson became the first tenants in the new Studio Building built by Lawren Harris and Dr. James MacCallum. Jackson's stay was brief on that occasion, but the building became home for a number of the artists including J. E. H. MacDonald and Frank Carmichael. They were launching the first truly Canadian art movement.

The 100th anniversary of Tom Thomson's birth at Claremont was celebrated in 1977 throughout Canada. Thomson's early years were spent in rural Ontario without access to formal art education. The young man moved to Seattle for a brief stay after the turn of the century but returned to Toronto to the commercial art firm of Grip Limited where providentially he met Lismer, MacDonald, Carmichael, Johnston and Varley.

In 1914, Thomson abandoned his job to paint in the wilds of Algonquin Park while supplementing his income with seasonal jobs as guide and forest ranger. Skilled in canoeing and woodlore, he penetrated remote areas of the forest and rapidly distilled their moods in gemlike pigment on small birch panels.

When snows were deep and temperatures low, Thomson returned to Toronto until the spring breakup began. He preferred the shack located behind the Studio Building for his quarters paying Lawren Harris rent of one dollar a month. Tom settled in with spartan furnishings, a stove, a bunk in the loft, and he built the easel on which his great canvases were painted. Tom Thomson's shack was moved to Kleinburg in 1962 and stands preserved on the grounds of the McMichael Canadian Collection.

Thomson and Jackson influenced each other, as Jackson recalled,

FRANK CARMICHAEL
Scrub Oaks and Maples   1935
60.5 x 78.5

TOM THOMSON
Sunrise   1916-17   21.6 x 26.7

TOM THOMSON
Summer Day   1915-16
21.6 x 26.8

I supplied the school learning and practical methods of working and helped Tom to realize the dreams which were stored within the treasure house, while my debt to him is almost that of a new world, the north country and a truer artist's vision, because as an artist he was rarely gifted.

Camping at Algonquin with Thomson in the fall of 1914, Jackson painted his memorable *Red Maple* at the Oxtongue River while Thomson's joyous use of colour fully emerged and his style took wings. The artist seized the fleeting colour of the sunset and slashed the pigment to the board with a rapid stroke. Varley was moved to comment that Thomson was becoming "a new cubist."

Harris, Lismer and particularly J. E. H. MacDonald exerted strong guidance on Thomson in areas of design and composition. MacDonald's skies were seldom equalled, while Thomson's own glorious clouds began to appear in the 1915-16 years surpassing those of any Canadian artist.

In the last year of his life, Thomson's panels became more abstracted. *Autumn Birches*, 1916 and *Autumn Colour*, 1916 invite speculation as to how far he would have moved in this direction had he lived a longer life.

Thomson's first purchased canvas brought him $250, a highly acceptable price at that time, but his work sold spasmodically. The bulk of over 500 small oil panels painted in his brief career sold after his death as did almost all his major canvases. *The Jack Pine* was purchased by the National Gallery of Canada for $750. Now his work commands the highest prices of any Canadian artist. Among the relatively few canvases of his lifetime, *Summer Shore, Georgian Bay* stands as one of Thomson's great achievements as indeed his small oil panels remain as tributes to his genius.

LAWREN HARRIS
Mt. Lefroy   1930
132.7 x 153.3

J. E. H. MacDONALD
Leaves in the Brook   1919
53.8 x 66.3

12

Thomson drowned at Canoe Lake, in Algonquin Park on July 8th, 1917 before his fortieth birthday. The familiar area was a second home to the expert woodsman and canoeist and naturally questions arose concerning the cause of his death. It remains shrouded in mystery. Films, books and legend immortalize Thomson in Canadian lore, and his panels are treasures of our artistic heritage.

Thomson's death devastated his friends, and they placed a moving epitaph on the memorial cairn at Canoe Lake:

> *. . . He lived humbly but passionately with the wild. It made him brother to all untamed things of nature. It drew him apart and revealed itself wonderfully to him. It sent him out from the woods only to show these revelations through his art; and it took him to itself at last.*

The friends were widely separated by the first World War at the time of Thomson's death. Jackson, wounded in action, remained overseas. Despondent upon receiving the tragic news, he wrote to MacDonald that in the north country Thomson was "the guide, the interpreter and we the guests partaking of his hospitality so generously given." Jackson concluded, "I am going to play the game again Jim, and forget myself in work, if they only give me freedom enough."

In the months before the end of the War, Harris and Mac-Donald together with Johnston discovered the Algoma country in northwestern Ontario. It was a rugged land of breath-taking beauty with lakes and rivers deeply gouged into the terrain. Rocky shields and spectacular waterfalls interrupted the miles of primeval forest.

Algoma became a significant turning point for MacDonald, Harris, Jackson, Johnston and Arthur Lismer over the next few years, as they worked with new freedom and vitality resulting in a prodigious output that provided the basis for the first Group exhibition.

Lawren Harris arranged for the men to accompany him into that "veritable paradise." It was an exciting time judging from his letters. They travelled in a boxcar rented from the Algoma Central Railway, and they enthusiastically transformed it into their home. Outfitted with bunks, a stove and other necessities, a moose skull and painted Christmas tree for decoration, the boxcar also contained a hand-car and a canoe to take them into wilderness territory away from their sidings. The boxcar was uncoupled from the train at appropriate locations where the surroundings presented a new challenge.

MacDonald, the amateur poet philosopher and admirer of Thoreau and Walt Whitman, Harris with his theosophy, Jackson and his down to earth humour and Lismer's optimistic view of life must have contributed to lively discussions around the fire long into the crisp autumn nights.

It was in Algoma that Jim MacDonald did his finest work. The canvases, *Leaves in the Brook* and *Algoma Forest*, now in the McMichael Collection, present a kaleidoscope of colour but MacDonald revelled in the small vigorous sketches of this period and they remain sumptuous in their brilliance. The artist's gentle, sensitive nature seemed to belie the strength so evident in his work.

Frank Johnston's *Patterned Hillside*, painted when he was with the Group in Algoma, demonstrates that he was one with them for that period. The quality of his work displayed the same scintillating colour favoured by his friends.

ARTHUR LISMER
Bright Land   1938
83.0 x 103.0

A. Y. Jackson's master canvas, *First Snow, Algoma,* was the artist's favourite painting among the vast output of his lifetime. The panel was painted on the 1919 boxcar trip, his first exposure to the rugged country of Algoma. It was a chilling time with the first snow swirling above the ground. Jackson brightened the solemn terrain with the dash of crimson of the stunted mountain ash. He captured the vast panorama drawing the eyes over the planes into the distance, conveying his eagerness to travel beyond the horizon and explore.

The artist's strongest work was created during the 1920's and 1930's, while his later painting emphasized strong curving strokes married with his keen perception of light. Jackson favoured warm earth tones and found inspiration from the patches of snow lingering on the brown earth as winter gave way to spring. A. Y. was a remarkable recorder of our land probably travelling throughout more of Canada than any person. He shared his travels not only through paintings but through the writing of amusing letters to his friends and irate epistles to newspapers. In his entertaining autobiography published in 1958, *A Painter's Country,* Jackson spoke of his trips throughout the country defending or advancing his views on the state of Canadian art.

Propelled by the enthusiastic Lawren Harris and J. E. H. MacDonald, the Group of Seven formed in Toronto in 1920. The artists preferred an informal association without constitution or minutes. They mounted their first exhibition that year at the Art Museum of Toronto with 114 submissions from the Group together with paintings by their friends, Hewton, Pilot and Robinson. Frank Carmichael designed the Group of Seven logo for this initial exhibition, although they adopted more elaborate versions in subsequent catalogues. Carmichael's original logo is reproduced on the back cover of this book.

In the first catalogue, the Group of Seven firmly stated that

A. J. CASSON
Fog Clearing   1929
Watercolour
43.0 x 50.8 (sight)

an Art must grow and flower in the land before the country will be a real home for its people.

What would the reaction be to these vibrant paintings directly inspired by the land? Harris's foreword indicated the Group invited adverse criticism but "Indifference is the greatest evil they have to contend with."

The newspaper accounts report praise for the artists and their work although this had not been the case with earlier exhibitions when they were referred to as "The Hot Mush School." With the passage of years, we have no way of assessing the extent of verbal disapproval or letters to the newspapers. Jackson repeatedly spoke of offensive criticism directed at the Group, most of it from Royal Canadian Academy members. He felt it had the immediate consequence of causing Frank Johnston's resignation.

In point of fact, Johnston received critical acclaim in that first show, and his *Fire Swept – Algoma* sold to the National Gallery for $750. As Johnston had a family with young children, it was important to him that his work be commercially viable. He moved to Winnipeg in 1922 and became principal of the Winnipeg School of Art. The artist began to direct his painting more to the taste of the public than towards the revolutionary trends favoured during the early Algoma years. During this period, Johnston became the most commercially successful member of the Group of Seven.

The selection of Group members as representatives of Canada for the 1924 Commonwealth Exhibition, at Wembly, England, produced considerable controversy. Although works were shown by artists from across Canada, some Group paintings had been chosen to the exclusion of more traditional Canadian works. British critics praised the Group members and other Canadian artists stating that their

F. H. VARLEY
Mountain Portage   1925
50.8 x 60.9

landscapes had distinctive character in subject and treatment. The artists were elated as the clippings began to appear and the Tate Gallery in London purchased an A. Y. Jackson canvas.

Canadian newspapers continued to report controversy over Group paintings. One headline in the Toronto Star 1925 read "Group Work Has Been Described as Hideous, Marvelous, Terrible and Also Magnificent." Another report referred to Group works "as a revelation of the Canadian soul."

By 1930, the Group artists, no longer the cohesive band of the 20's, were following separate paths. Varley lived in Vancouver and Lismer travelled widely spending that summer in the Maritimes. Jackson planned his second visit to the high Arctic and convinced Lawren Harris to accompany him.

Jackson and Harris thrived on the rigorous journey aboard the government supply ship, "Beothic," as the old ship ploughed through treacherous ice floes and howling gales. The awesome land of the far north inspired interesting painting from Jackson and monumental work from Harris, such as *Icebergs, Davis Strait*.

Despite the Group's diversification and talk of dissolution, Edwin Holgate of Quebec joined in 1931 and exhibited in their shows. Holgate's memorable portraits and figure studies were conceived with the thoughtful consideration and strength found in his landscapes. The painting *Fishermen's Houses*, is representative of Holgate's mastery of the landscape.

While Group artists were best known for landscapes, Holgate, FitzGerald and Varley were Canadians of that period to paint the figure. Varley captured his subjects with remarkable sensitivity, while Holgate excelled in his portraits such as *Ludovine*, in The National Gallery.

EDWIN HOLGATE
The Cellist   1923
129.5 x 97.8

Months before the artists ended their association as a Group, "the Painter of the Prairies," Lemoine FitzGerald of Manitoba, accepted membership in June, 1932. He had exhibited with the Group in the past, but he was not destined to do so as a member.

In the fall of 1932, when he was principal of the Ontario College of Art in Toronto, J. E. H. MacDonald died. *Goat Range, Rocky Mountains* in the McMichael Collection is one of his last two canvases. His mastery of design had successfully reduced the panorama of the Rockies to its essence. MacDonald's panels and canvases rich with vibrant colour epitomized the Group of Seven's aim of painting their country in a distinctive Canadian manner.

With the death of MacDonald and the separation of the members by geography and diverging interests, dissolution was inevitable. Shortly thereafter, the Group, joined by colleagues became charter members of the Canadian Group of Painters, a direct extension of the Group of Seven. The expanded membership of 28 was composed of men and women across Canada including contemporaries Emily Carr and David Milne.

In retrospect, although known as a group of seven, the artists were clearly men of divergent personalities. Lawren Harris was the driving force. He continued to take the initiative not only throughout their formative years but after. Although he went through periods of solitary introspection, Harris conversely showed amazing energy and consistently organized and carried through ventures with boundless enthusiasm. He had shown a spirit of adventure hiking through the Austrian Tyrol as a student, and it was perhaps there he discovered his passion for mountain solitude. The artist continued to find a sense of spiritual renewal emanating from the mountain environment.

FRANK JOHNSTON
Patterned Hillside   1918
26.7 x 33.6

23

L. L. FITZGERALD
The Little Plant   1947
60.9 x 46.4

After his student years, the young Harris travelled throughout Palestine by camel as an illustrator for Harper's Magazine. On to Minnesota for brief visits to logging camps again on assignment. What a background in living for a young artist! It stirred a sense of mobility and restlessness that possessed him throughout his career. Harris investigated an area, a subject in depth and then moved on to a new consideration. The manifestation of his kineticism does not appear with regularity until his explorations of the non-objective from the 1930's until the end of his career.

In several of his paintings of houses, particularly those of Glace Bay, Nova Scotia, there is evidence of his later development of the abstract and the psychic, reflections of the German and Scandinavian influences encountered during his student years.

The mystical link between man and nature became a force driving Harris to explore his deepest spiritual concepts creatively not only through painting but in poetry and essays. Theosophy was of consuming interest to the artist as with Mondrian and Kandinsky. The Russian Kandinsky's, *Concerning the Spiritual in Art*, deeply influenced Harris to adopt symbolic colour into facets of his work.

Harris's 1930 masterpiece, *Icebergs, Davis Straits*, is a realistic perception of a phenomenon of nature, majestic bergs emerging through pools of colour, their depths hidden from view. Or it may be interpreted on the plain of Harris's philosophical explorations of the bridge between man and nature, mystic light from the source illumes the bergs and mankind with the spiritual force significant to the artist.

Frederick Varley shared Harris's interest in the mystical. Born in Britain, he came to Canada in 1912 following years of training as an artist. Varley returned to the continent in 1918 during the first World War as a Canadian Army war artist. His vivid narrative commentaries in his paintings *For What?* and *Some Day The People Will Return* bypass the usual documentary and indelibly impress the viewer with the artist's sense of outrage and the futility of war.

On his return to Canada, Varley found portrait commissions and teaching the only profitable areas open to him in Canadian art. Certainly Varley preferred people to trees, but his landscapes reveal the artist's close affinity with nature. Varley merged the human form into landscapes in such paintings as *Indians Crossing Georgian Bay*, 1920 and *Mountain Portage*, 1925.

Varley's portraits of women have a mystical, often enigmatic quality. Over the years, he became engrossed in the religions of the East which inspired him to use colours with spiritual qualities. His unusual colour concepts continued to develop particularly during the British Columbia years. Varley's sensitivity enabled him to perceive the subtlety of colour change in nature's infinite variety of light and reflections.

His lack of discipline in his personal life led to a bohemian existence and occasional rifts with his colleagues and friends. Varley is acknowledged as Canada's greatest portrait artist and a master colourist, but to many, his drawings are his finest achievement.

In Arthur Lismer's mind, painting and teaching were inseparable. Painting became his avocation with teaching a profession that involved him for life. Before he became a student apprentice in Sheffield, England, young Lismer discovered the joys of sketching and his pencil was seldom still. His strong sense of humour is revealed in his aptitude for caricatures and cartoons which filled pages of innumerable sketch books throughout his career. Children instinctively felt at ease with him perhaps because of his humour

TOM THOMSON
Wildflowers 1917
21.7 x 26.8

TOM THOMSON
Moonlight and Birches   1916-17   22.0 x 27.0

TOM THOMSON
Snow Shadows   1915   21.2 x 26.7

and inquisitiveness, qualities which led to his laurels as an educator.

Lismer successfully pioneered art classes for children in Toronto and later Montreal, and he achieved an international reputation for his work. The artist insisted that the young people's interest could be captured through inspiration and the experience of visualizing form. Their technical skills could follow under relaxed unfettered conditions. He was invited to share his philosophy of teaching in South Africa, Australia and New Zealand and later as an educator at New York's Columbia and Montreal's McGill universities.

Lismer spent his last years in Montreal, a familiar figure with flowing white hair and pockets bulging with intriguing objects. He died there in 1969 in his eighty-fourth year, a life of fulfillment behind him.

Lismer left an impressive legacy of drawings, many executed with the reed pens he carved. His ability to laugh at himself, the Group and their encounters, and indeed the ridiculous in almost any situation, provides a delightful view of this remarkable man. He was prophetic in his humorous cartoon showing the Group of Seven cemetery for he is now buried there with his friends Jackson, Harris, Varley and Johnston on the grounds of the McMichael Collection close to the paintings that are monuments to their vision.

For many years Franklin Carmichael was less known to the public than his work deserved. This is changing, for today Carmichael's paintings are among the most sought after of Canadian works.

He was born at Orillia, Ontario in 1890 and apprenticed at Grip Limited, Toronto, in the same year as Lismer joined the firm. His work at this company led to an early association with the men later to form the Group of Seven.

A. Y. JACKSON
Valley of the Gouffre River   1933
64.5 x 82.2

Carmichael continued developing his technical skills at the Ontario College of Art and later at Antwerp, in Belgium.

Carmichael depicted the pioneer village and the isolation of the remote country dwelling with painting imparting a quiet, yet lived-in quality to the hamlets. On the other hand, he captured a majestic sense of the eternal far removed from man in his works of the wilderness. The artist's confident sense of design is always in control of his impressive compositions.

Carmichael's art was highly disciplined and he demanded perfection not only from himself and his students but from his protegé, A. J. Casson. Casson enjoys referring to Carmichael as his mentor and the person who introduced him to the men of the Group at the Arts and Letters Club, Toronto.

Carmichael travelled to the north shore of Lake Superior on several occasions from 1925 to 1928. He confined his painting to Ontario and after 1930, he sketched when possible in the unspoiled wilderness above Manitoulin Island at the LaCloche Hills. Carmichael found the land he had been looking for.

Carmichael and Casson, together with Fred Brigden, co-founded the Canadian Society of Painters in Water Colour in 1926. Watercolour held a particular appeal for them unlike other members of the Group, and the two friends worked equally in that medium and oils. They hoped to bring watercolour into prominence through exhibitions and the Society's success fulfilled their early expectations.

Carmichael and Casson used watercolour with a boldness rarely seen in Canada. At first, it must have appeared as a formidable challenge to present landscapes in watercolour with the vibrancy and power of the Group oils. In their hands, watercolour attained a visual impact of its own.

TOM THOMSON
Tea Lake Dam   1916
21.4 x 26.3

31

Carmichael's inspired *Mirror Lake* transports the viewer, leading the eye from the depth of the lake into the hills beyond.

In 1945, when he was Vice-Principal of the Ontario College of Art, Franklin Carmichael died at the age of fifty-five. *Scrub Oaks and Maples* is among his works in the McMichael Collection which stand in summary tribute to his artistry.

Born in Toronto, the young Alfred Casson began a career leading to thirty-two years as a commercial designer and executive. He found the cost of oils prohibitive when he began to paint in 1916 whereas watercolours were both inexpensive and convenient to carry on his treks. Casson's interest in watercolour continued for over fifteen years until on a fall sketching trip it rained day after day – a disaster for a watercolourist. Casson promptly switched his allegiance to oils.

The artist has gained a reputation as a recorder of the early Ontario houses and villages which are rapidly disappearing. Over the years, he has sought to capture the curious eerie feeling of stillness, "quieter than quiet" as he says. This mood pervades the paintings *Maynooth* and *Houses, Bancroft*.

A blue cloudless day is a blank day for Casson, who prefers the challenge of a lively sky with an abundance of clouds and shadows. At Superior, Casson found these ideal conditions. *Fog Clearing* reveals an awesome moment of great beauty when the mist rises to reveal the undulant hills below. Casson's rural homespun paintings of the thirties fled before his radical change of style in the mid-forties. He experimented with geometric planes of light and superimposing images, a reflection of cubism lightly tinged with the surreal. They were well received but from this work, the artist moved towards a greater simplicity with emphasis on pattern and restricted colour schemes.

FRANK CARMICHAEL
Mirror Lake   1929
Watercolour   44.6 x 54.3 (sight)

33

Casson's work appears in outstanding collections in Canada and the United States. Following Holgate's death in 1977, Casson remains the living member of the Group of Seven, the conservative of the revolutionary group.

Over sixty years have passed since Tom Thomson painted his first canvas *A Northern Lake* in 1913, and he introduced Jackson and Lismér to the plethora of the Ontario wilderness. The artists sought to distill the image of Canada and to awaken the pride and confidence of Canadian people in their own creativity and environment. The Group's 1920 catalogue stated

> *. . . the greatness of a country depends upon three things: "its Words, its Deeds, and its Art." Recognizing that Art is an essential quality in human existence they will welcome and support any form of Art expression that sincerely interprets the spirit of a nation's growth.*

In the early years of this century, the artists struggled with like-minded people to turn Canadians from attitudes of a colonial people to those of proud nationalists. Eric Brown, Director of the National Gallery advocated a policy to "aid the development of Canada's art", and he enthusiastically supported the Group's work from the beginning. Canadian writers were determined to create a literature reflecting their nationalistic development, and publications including the Canadian Forum and the Canadian Historical Review evolved. E. J. Pratt, made a break-through in verse with his clear imagery of the people, the work and the face of Canada.

The self-confidence of the 1920's was boosted by Canada's spirited economic expansion. As the northern resources developed with advancing technology and transportation, Group of Seven artists were lured further into the northern wilderness as were the prospectors, engineers and bush pilots. Canada asserted herself politically loosening ties with

J. E. H. MacDONALD
Artist's Home and Orchard   1927
21.5 x 26.3

Britain, sending her first diplomatic representatives abroad and controlling her own foreign policy. She was feeling the stirring of her new spirit of nationhood. Although change was occurring, traditionalists still had a dominant voice in the world of art.

Towards the end of the decade, the Group of Seven had made their statement and prepared to follow separate paths. Together with Tom Thomson, they had broken the trail for the generations to follow. Their paintings gave meaning in visual terms to nebulous images of Canada and stand in testament to the grandeur of the country and their inspirations.

From 1976 to 1978, Group of Seven and Tom Thomson paintings toured in the longest exhibition of Canadian art undertaken abroad. Opening in Glasgow, 44 canvases and sketches from the McMichael Canadian Collection then appeared in Edinburgh, Aberdeen, London, Washington, Munich, Bonn and Hamburg. The renowned Hermitage at Leningrad was followed by Kiev and Moscow. The exhibition travelled to Oslo, Norway and the National Gallery of Ireland, Dublin and concluded at the Art Gallery at Kilkenny Castle in June of 1978. The tour was under the auspices of the Government of Canada and the Province of Ontario.

Nearly half a century ago, Jackson jovially prophesied the Group would not be remembered as rebels but rather as "those old academic Johnnies." As Paul Richards recently stated in the Washington Post

> . . . *but it is not their modernism that moves us now. Rather it is their passion, the enthusiasm with which they painted the wilderness they loved.*

TOM THOMSON
Summer Shore   c. 1916
72.5 x 77.5

LAWREN HARRIS
Early Houses   1913
26.9 x 33.5

LAWREN HARRIS
Eclipse Sound and Bylot Island   1930
30.2 x 38.0

LAWREN HARRIS
Icebergs, Davis Strait   1930
121.9 x 152.4

LAWREN HARRIS
Pic Island 1924
121.9 x 152.4

F. H. VARLEY
Girl in Red   1926
53.5 x 52.0

ARTHUR LISMER
Forest, Algoma 1922
71.1 x 91.4

A. J. CASSON
Pike Lake   1929
Watercolour
42.2 x 50.7 (sight)

A. J. CASSON
Summer Hillside, Kamaniskeg   1945
50.7 x 61.1

LAWREN HARRIS
Montreal River 1920
26.9 x 34.8

A. J. CASSON
Kleinburg 1929
23.9 x 28.5

TOM THOMSON
Snow in the Woods   1916
21.7 x 27.2

FRANK CARMICHAEL
October Gold 1922
120.0 x 98.7

A. Y. JACKSON
Houses, St. Urbain c. 1934
21.6 x 26.7

A. Y. JACKSON
Nellie Lake   1933
76.9 x 81.4

J. E. H. MacDONALD
Young Maples, Algoma   1918
21.6 x 26.6

A. J. CASSON
White Pine 1957
76.2 x 101.6

A. Y. JACKSON
Skeena Crossing 1926
54.0 x 66.8

FRANK CARMICHAEL
A Northern Silver Mine   1930
101.6 x 121.9

53

A. Y. JACKSON
Church at St. Urbain 1931
54.0 x 66.6

F. H. VARLEY
Stormy Weather, Georgian Bay 1920
21.6 x 26.7

A. Y. JACKSON
Grey Day, Laurentians   1933
54.0 x 66.2

EDWIN HOLGATE
Fishermen's Houses   c. 1933
51.0 x 61.2   57

A. Y. JACKSON
The Red Maple   1914
21.7 x 26.9

J. E. H. MacDONALD
Algoma Forest   1919
21.4 x 26.5

ARTHUR LISMER
Evening Silhouette   1926
60   32.5 x 40.5

L. L. FITZGERALD
The Harvester   1921
69.0 x 62.2

F. H. VARLEY
Negro Head   1940
40.2 x 30.6

J. E. H. MacDONALD
Goat Range, Rocky Mountains 1932
53.8 x 66.0

CREDITS

Design: Alfred J. Casson
Photography: Hugh W. Thompson
Text: Jeanne L. Pattison
Front Cover: Tom Thomson, Black Spruce in Autumn
Printing: Matthews Ingham and Lake Inc.